T0198032

BREAD SEX TREES

poetry

ALIX KLINGENBERG

For my family, ancestral and chosen.

with all these keys and flowers

you'd think I might have some

clue how to open.

FULLY LOST

We begin with the ground,
with earth.

Roots, caves, safety.

We begin with breath,
with rest, with creation,
with clay.

We begin at the beginning,
which is possibly the middle or even the end,
but definitely not the sky.

We will start with the burial,
a ceremony of digging in.

We begin on the inside,
alone, with our thoughts,
an exploration of our inner landscapes,
our body gardens.

Where have you been hiding?
Are you finally, fully lost?

BREAD | SEX | TREES

I keep thinking about bread
the soft way it breathes
the smell of yeast and flour and salt
the way the ingredients become liquid
then solid, alive
and full of sustenance.

I keep thinking about mornings
in your bed, the sun streaming in
you bring me the French press and
leave me alone to write.
I've never known someone
who could make silence sound
like adoration.

I keep thinking about roots
underground pushing and tangling.
The way trees are supported by forces
invisible to the sparrows in the branches,
the way the earth is teeming with life
under the surface,

the way everything
that lasts takes its sweet time becoming.
Rising, resting, and rising again,

like bread
like sex
like trees.

JANUARY

When my head is sore
and my heart is doing that thing
where it aches
for no discernible
reason,

when I feel cold
and hard
and solemn,

I return to the earth
and let her remind me
that rest (cold and solemn)
is what winter is for.

IT WAS THE YEAR

the rain fell
like bells on the
rooftop. The year I forgot
the exact way
my father said my name,
only that he broke

it into almost 3 syllables instead of 2.
It was the year the car
broke down on the highway
and you walked 4 miles
to the nearest exit
while I waited in the car

under blankets, wondering if I'd ever get home.
Wondering who would feed my cat.

It was the year I outgrew
all my clothes
and not in the good way.
In the way that every magazine warns you about,
in the way that made me feel
gigantic and also invisible.

It was the year I couldn't cry,
all the tears had been used to drown out
the sound of loneliness and fill bathtubs
with salt water and lavender.

The year I stopped wondering if you
would come back.
The year the crops grew tall while I grew
wise and sad.

TELL ME WHAT COULD HAPPEN

We could drive to the middle
of the cornfield
and kiss
under the rabbit moon.

We could let our hands find every
curve in the dark
mouths covering mouths
hair
skin
buttons.

We could stay very still
in the place between
touching   and not touching.

We could stop for a while,
let our insides
coalesce into dark matter,
dense and inescapable.

Find a hotel bed
an airplane
a train
we could shatter into slivers,
broken mirrors in the bathtub,

we could melt each other down
for parts

rebuilt again into unimaginable
machines of fire
burn the whole world down.

I can't get the smoke
of your gaze out of my hair
and every piece of me reeks
of you in the morning.

AT LAST

I'm pretty sure
this is what love
was supposed to look like
all along.

Like falling into step
with sanity.
Like holding on to
a piece of yourself
walking around in
another body.

Like so little concrete
and so much sand.

I SMILE INSTEAD

I want to scream
like a goat
into the yawning expanse
of your mouth.
Lean all my weight
against the tree
and watch it crush the house.

Take all the words
you used to make me small
and force you to eat them
behind the woodshed.

I smile instead.
I flip my hair
and decide to lose
ten pounds instead.

I explain myself rationally,
draw up a chart in
three colors instead.
Ask if that makes sense
instead.

I am barely contained.

My sanity is held in
by the thinnest membrane.
If I press too hard,

I will give it all away.

I don't know how
to get angry enough, ya know?
Where do they teach you how to scream?

I tuck my wings away

so you won't see how far

I could fly without you.

I BREAK THINGS:

dishes/ hearts/ rules.

I mend things:
time/ space/ buttons.

I move things:
furniture/ people/ priorities.

I pull things:
apart/ inside/ down.

ache until the pieces align
try again and again
to be more than one thing.

I am learning
to alter my identity
with a razor-sharp
seam ripper
instead of coming after it
with the subtlety of a woodchipper
or the precision of a house fire.

PINK FLAGS

I am always getting
into cars for soft
candy and coming
out with loose teeth.

You smell like
clean shirts

and another way
to forget myself.

RUINS

You spoke and my walls
turned to mud,
just earth and water
and an open path
right to the center of me.

Now I am a land unguarded
and you...

you are nowhere to be found.

ENTANGLED

I have let you all the way in,
formed organs around you.

Layers and layers of skin and bone,
your fingers have access to my left ventricle
and the muscles under my cheekbones.

You move inside me and I am remade,
sinew and sensuality

love that feels like maybe, just maybe,
I don't have to do everything alone.

QUANTUM LOVE

I wish you understood
what my love meant.
How it never was a particle
or a wave, but somehow
both at once.

Once created it could never be
destroyed, only transformed.

I've lit up cities with it since
you disappeared.
Wrote your name
in colored lights on skyscrapers
so the birds
might tell you where I am.

So the stars might
whisper in your ear
that yours is still the only
face I see when I close my
eyes against the setting sun.

DANGEROUS THINGS TO UNLEARN

I need to learn
to stop dimming my magic
so that you might outshine me.
Why do I do that?
Why do you let me?

UNDERBELLY

I am having dark and heated thoughts
red lights and leather booths
that stick to my bare skin.

I miss the taste of whiskey
and the smell of your neck.

I want everything I cannot have,
crave everything that pulls me
away from safety.

CONVICTED

If I were brought before a jury
they would convict me without question.
I have always been a harlot,
give me all the scarlet letters, baby,
they'll make me easier to spot
on a crowded train platform.

In my defense, I wasn't touched
enough as a child.
I've never known a love
that didn't come later.

I remember being 12 or maybe 14
and seeing the way men looked at me from
their big rigs. I would open my legs slightly
in the car for them to see,

sometimes they would honk their horns
and I knew right then,
I had power.

One time (actually it's been many times)
I made a man break his word
just to prove I could.
I reminded him that he said
he would never cheat on his girlfriend
while he was inside me.

The prosecution would like to

remind the reader that I don't
remember his name.

When I was 17, I turned Andy against God,
just for a couple minutes,
satisfying only in theory.
In my defense, his mother
put ketchup on tacos.
In my defense, his God
was written by committee.

Yes, if I were brought before a jury
I would be convicted without question.
No doubt. No shadow.

ENOUGH

Even though I still
have your hands I sometimes
miss your face. I often

wonder exactly where our
levity went. I often
go to bed instead
of staying up and chatting with you
because I can feel the way I

can't quite maintain interest
the way I used to and it
scares me. And even though
I know we've spent two

years in fear for our lives,
stuck inside with no
source of fun and no time
alone, I'm afraid

I've lost something I may never
find again. A sense of what is
enough.

When will it feel like I get
enough praise,
enough money, love,
intimacy.

When will enough people
have read my words, when
will I have seen
enough of the world.

And sometimes when I stare
at you I worry I will
throw everything I love
away, out of a desire to
know

just how much agony
I can withstand,
just to know how it
feels to lose
enough.

FEBRUARY

Oh, how I long
for mint and honey,
for dancing and fireflies,
for hands just lightly touching my hands
as we reach for the
same
ripe
melon.

SANCTUARY

She fled to the woods
to find dark branches
reaching toward
such soft light.

The mushrooms
chatting at the edge
of the sanctuary.

And in treetops
birds and squirrels
dropped acorns
to mark the passing of time.

As if flutter and chatter
weren't prayer enough,
the wind came in with a sigh
to wash away any symptoms
of grief.

Everything falls away
and eventually
everything re-arrives.

I KEEP CHOOSING PINK

pink phone
pink laptop
pink notebook
pink sky
I draw pink hearts on my wrist
I pink my tongue
I taste the bud
pink roses become
prom corsages/white Cadillac
I picture my dad singing
and a wave of grief comes forward,
a pink wave, not quite red,
less harsh, more soft,
like mountains in the background,
a happy little grief,
I can feel the way I dodge the avalanche
make new ways around the pain.
sepia photographs from the '70s,
before I was born
I think I missed something good,
soft pink light turned '80s neon
I was born at a time of overconsumption
your overconsumption
and so I watch the snow
turn a pink kind of blue,
and I set down pink words
on the pink page.

like blood
but with more white.

If I learned one thing
last year it's that
even true love can
walk away.

That men will break
their own hearts
for a chance to be good
and women would throw
everything away
for a chance to be whole.

SAW RED

pools of blood on picnic
table. camp nurse was in the
pool. running uphill toward chlorine,
cut grass, three kinds of green.
my head
spinning
my injured hand
waving wildly,
stop
hurting
can't stop
shaking
the blood loose
remove the pain
with erratic action,
wet sleeve,
on knees

Everything black.

I leave pieces
        of myself
                everywhere I go.

I have learned
to stave the flow of blood
with my own steady pressure.

I have learned

not to run up hills
chasing safety.

but I am, at my core,
someone who will recklessly
carve a name
into wood with a dull pocket knife —
bleed everywhere,
stain the world with red,
for a chance at a love that lasts.

A STRANGE INHERITANCE

Sometimes I wonder at my choice to become a mother,
so unwilling to give myself over to the task of
ignoring my own desires in favor of his.
His small face can tell that I am only half in it sometimes.
And I don't have to wonder how that feels.

I take his hand in those moments,
hoping a touch will connect us
when words and actions cannot.

And I know that one day he will wish
I was more and also less...
like every other man I've ever loved.
But I can only be enough for myself.

There is a strange entanglement of mother/child.
The strange way I made him with my body
and sustained him with my own milk.
He is of me and not even remotely me.

I look at him and wish I had a better legacy to leave,
something more than this
inevitable passing down of loneliness.

HOUSE HUNTING WITH YOUR BONES

Walk through with blue booties on
so as to not scuff
hardwood, new countertops,
this one has a spice rack and
I am wracked with a feeling that
I will never feel at home.

That no amount of space
will ever be enough to quench
my craving for freedom.
But maybe I will have a
little room,
a place to do puzzles
and a fireplace that turns on
with a light switch and
a little burst of "foomp."

Maybe I will find the right
square footage to
keep my feet out of my mouth
and my desire to run screaming
for the woods at bay
for another 15 years.

Enough to see you through,
enough to watch you grow
through the door of my
new office where I hide
from the realities of the life

I built from more than stone
and brick.

And, what is this, stucco?
Shiplap accent wall
and I am shipwrecked
in a sea of apathy
and a sense that I have
lost all semblance of reality.

We will dwell in the bones
of your mother's death
and every exposed beam
will remind me of the year
you couldn't touch her hands
or say goodbye

and how I couldn't cry
because then I would have to admit
that she was worth more to me
this way...

HOUSE RULES

In this house we are painters and poets,
heathens and hideaways,
lovers of secrets
and keepers of the old stories.

We are readers, scholars, and skeptics,
sarcastic nihilists who make meaning
from warm, sidelong glances.

We live in ideas and dwell
in the impossible contradictions
of hope and despair,
of love and inevitable heartbreak,
of life and losing.

In this house we are seekers of
things that feel true and
find romance in the deep honesty
of all that is unknown.

I SEARCHED FOR HOME FOR A LONG, LONG TIME

Always lost, always wandering,
fingering the wall for secret keyholes
fingering the wall for anything round

      And finally

I built a home within myself —
      made of poetry and longing

      of early mornings and burning twigs
      made of deep sighs and long kisses

      made of line drawings and legos
      of wildflowers and skeleton keys
      that unlock every door when
      the time is right.

      Of brightly colored paper
      and pieces of dreams.

I carry home with me now.
Mine to share with whom
I choose.

I know it's scary,
but choose you.
The real you
the whole you
the you you meet in the dark at 2am
the you you sing to in the car.
Choose her.
The rest will come.

MARCH

I hear the birds
greeting spring with
rough winter throats
and breezes so warm
they scare themselves,

shock the trees into
blooming too early.
I warm my hands
on the memory of who
I thought you were.

Some loves aren't meant
to last the winter.

UNPACKING

I am a room
cleared in the center
and cluttered around the edges,
boxes unpacked,
ideas unfinished,
lives on hold,
forgotten and dusty.

I take you out
like a faded photograph
and press my face
to your memory,

only people who
promise to stay forever
never do.

GRANDMOTHER QUILTS

Crawl inside my skin
and bear the wild world
in my tender animal suit.

Tell me how it feels, love.
Are you closer to the sun?
Do harsh words whip through you
like March winds without a coat?

Do you try, like I do,
to wrap people around you
like grandmother quilts?
Never
quite
enough.

Does it hurt for you, too?
Tell me I'm not alone.
At least tell me that.

He looks at me
with child eyes,
not young
but innocent.

He still believes
love is enough.

(And maybe, just maybe, it is.)

IN MEMORIAM:

The man had a way with unusual harmonies,
going high when most would go low.
He got dressed downstairs, no shame
about his oversized belly or his whitey tighties.
He broke my name into three syllables somehow "yyyyaaalix,"
a drawl so thick it
sounded like a yell.
He used to keep money in his socks,
had a system for the quarter slots.
A system for everything.
I once tied his laces together when he was
asleep and he fell with a horrifying thud
on the bedroom floor.
I'm told he jumped into a hot tub
to save me, shoes on.
He once left me alone and sleeping
at age 6, went to the bar down the street.
Found me at his mother's house in the morning.
I'd walked there alone.
We set off the fireworks in the backyard,
went fishing, played chess.
Though he broke his vows a million times
I thought we'd sing together again. Maybe.
If he lived long enough.
If he'd lived long enough.

TEMPEST

I am moon and mountain weather,
dark sky and white bones,
bleached teeth on black beaches.

I am sand creature,
dissolve & harden—
devastation maker,
stone monster crustacean

though it may take
500 years to
wash away this
ocean heart . . .

I am leather jacket skin
zipped over melted rib.
Grit in teeth and
stick in wings,

I promise
I will never make
promises again.

CONSIDER THIS

Today I am leaving
and taking a trunk full of
feathered pillows and
gossamer undergarments.

I am a woman who has never lived alone
so maybe all I need is lingerie
and a way to sleep so my back
doesn't ache in the morning.

My jaw is always clenched
and I wonder what diving into a pool
of warm water would feel like
if I had no life to return to,

if diving into warm pools
and finding novel ways to dry off
was my entire plan for the day.

Hang lace panties from the
willow tree and harmonize
with the sound of water
dripping from black cotton.

I do believe I need very little:
just a way to stay soft,

just a way to carve out moments
when I don't feel like this life

is racing toward a finish line
of someone else's making.

I am like the salt
that dries from the sea

the evidence left behind
of enormous movement

the proof of tides.

BOTH/AND

All my life I have loved more than one thing.
Never able to choose between
the ferns and the maple,
the sun and the moon,
the ocean and the lake.
I am a woman of both/and.

I am a woman of many lives,
the men in my life can tell you.
They can tell you how I rise
a different person every day.

How each morning they must
meet me anew and discover
again how I take my coffee
or which version of me
they will walk to the edge
of the forest before they kiss me
and go off to work their normal work days.

All my life I have loved more than one thing
and I have been more than one thing.

I search the mirror for the multiplicities
and find an impossible dissonance
in the regularity of my eyebrows.
I seek a visual confirmation
of my many selves, some way
to ease the discontent of this singular body,
this unified life.

APRIL

Shedding the earth,
I wear nothing but the sky.
A cloak of night and the weight of everything,
no, everyone who died this year.
I write them on my wrists
and smell the syllables like
lavender and old spice.

I am exhausted, a ghost
returning from my midnight ride.
Climb down and let myself flow
through the cracks in the crocus blooms.
Dig down until I find the late spring ice
and drink of the coldest water
until I can see clearly again.

I BECOME RAIN

I am always becoming things like rain:
wet
falling hard
out of control

I become sand
soft and yielding,
piles and piles
of tiny warm stones
worn down by the water

the water I also become
whenever I need to breathe
more deeply —

I let the moon pull me around by the wrist.

If you will not take me as I am,
just let me know

I know how hard it is to love the rain
some days.

You make me question
everything beautiful
about myself,

and yet I run to you,
bleed out my colors
on your doorstep,

and beg for you to
feed me your darkness.

PINNACLE

If you ask me what's wrong,
I'll say it's the rain.

It's the way my body
moves in the morning light,
the slow walking through the backyard.

It's the growing list of to-dos
and appointments I've canceled.

It's a gnawing suspicion
I may be at my best right now

and everything else will fall away
from this pinnacle in an avalanche

of grief and destruction.
Perhaps it's that I'm happy
and that makes me sad.

THE STORM

You were a storm
come to wash my earth clean
of any delusions
that I can make anyone
love me.

I know this game, she thinks,
every time I lower my expectations
you lower your investment
until there is nothing.

love me freely, or not at all.

PAPER HANDS

My words tell a story
of who I am that surprises even me.
Unexpected anger and grief,
loud bursts of laughter,
and so many birds.

I've never thought of myself as a bird person.
I've never liked their black eyes.
But my words tell a deeper truth
of wings and fluttering
and a heart that's older than
any book ever written.

I write myself into the future.
I see fingers run over the raised ink
and watch the corners of the mouth for reaction.
I am starker on the page,
less forgiving, few smiles,
not nearly as many hair flips.

I am just a raw soul with paper hands
and a mind that's ready to tell the
daily news in black and white
and every shade of gray.

All I want
is to break
language into
birds.

BIRDS

I am my mother
I am my father
I am everyone I try not to become.

I am birds
I am birds
I am all the birds at once
moving in that chaotic, swirling
pattern through the ether.

I am the rain
I am the dirt becoming mud
I am the underside of the cat,
soft and unprotected.

I am disappearing into you,
into the dream of touch
into the pandemonium,
all wings and feathers
and flight.

WITCHCRAFT

I cast spells with eyelashes
and slightly upturned mouth corners.
With my ability to wait, like a rest in music,
for the right moment to present itself.

I cast spells with brutal honesty
made palatable with gentle touches
on your back near the spine,
where your ability to hear me lives.

I cast spells with my willingness to change,
my achingly open heart,
my desire to be good for you
and stay true to myself.

I cast these spells of authenticity
and can't believe the magical world
that has opened before me,
a cave of treasures,
golden piles of love
born of telling the truth softly.

REDACTED

There is something growing here:
a slowly rising audacity,

a kind of power
passed down through the cells
of magical women

and learned in dark corners
and hastily whispered secrets.

There is a knowledge brewing

cauldron-black and
velvet soft.

Dangerous ink-soaked wisdom

BEDTIME STORY

There's no rush,
but I want to wrap
my entire body around yours,
open your chest like a bedtime story,
and tell you every single
beautiful thing that I see.

How your energy flows
soft like a river
and tall like a pine tree,
green and pungent
electricity in the needles.

You are an entire atmosphere
of oxygen, somewhere I
can breathe more deeply,
somewhere I can be alive
and quietly, wildly, me.

REORIENTATION

I can feel myself moving away
from something I held at my center,
a core belief of some kind,
a golden ball of light I consumed
and let guide me from within.

I have no idea what it is,
what the piece is that no longer
serves as the point around which
I orbit, approval maybe, or achievement.

Instead I am gravitating toward a less
singular point in space, a collage,
a constellation of points in the
darkened sky of my soul.

It is not painful to let go
of what was, nor is it comfortable.
It is liminal — the space between
the jump and the land.

A GROWING AWARENESS OF TIME'S PASSING

Raindrops and red leaves
an urgency that rises
like geese over the tool shed

a knowing lateness

the air grows cold
and I am swept up in the dream
of darkness and rest

and all that must yet be done
before nightfall.

I crave your touch
but find myself in
window panes again.

I'll repeat myself until
I'm hoarse:
you can't find peace
by chopping off
the damaged parts
of yourself.
Grace only comes
when you love
yourself whole.

LAWN CULTURE

The neighbors eye
my pride flag with dismay
and wonder at my comings
and goings, stare with ire
at my wild lawn —

did you know that grass
does stop growing eventually?
It waves gently in the swaying breeze,
soft like boys who don't cut their hair.

Buying a home is only freedom
if you can stomach the concern
of your neighbors with a smile.

Walk quietly through the street
taking photographs
of the silhouetted leaves
making lace on the sidewalk
by the almost full moonlight.

I am always making
beauty of the shadows.

PASTEL DREAMS

Wisteria dreams
and drifting cloud thoughts.

I am blue lupine hands
in fields of Monet color.

Paint me in pastels
and remember
me like spring days,

effortless and soft.

MAY

These foggy mornings
remind me of you:
soft and sad
full of longing

heavy with the weight
of something unreleasable.

I've never loved anything
the way I love the fog.

Soft mysteries
like being lost
in your own backyard
and having to find
a new way home.

Summer rain and a grief
I don't know how to release.
I am so fucking jealous of the sky
for her ability to let it all go
and empty herself with a scream
that sets the air on fire.

JUNE

There is a quality
to June light that
just feels different
in the body:

less needed, more released.

Bodies photosynthesizing
a sacred tonic of
sweat and lemonade
into something resembling
transformation.

— How many ice cream sandwiches does it take
to leave this year behind us?

MANTRAS

I teach myself to read
the room, my body, my breath.
My own words become a mantra,
soothing ancient wounds
that flare up in colder weather,
like a bad knee.
You are safe.
You are loved.
You are enough.
You are free.
I teach my heart to slow.
I teach myself over and over again
that I am worthy of love.

LEARNING TO WAIT

I tell you I want to learn how to make bread
and you smile like it's simple,
just yeast and sugar, water, and flour,
salt to taste.
And I can feel my inadequacy
rise in my belly
like a sourdough.

Ingredients are simple,
chemistry is not.
And timing and heat,
the right kind of patience.
Patience, which is somehow
the sweat on your brow,
the ease of your lounging.
The taste of your fingertips —
there is never a need to hurry.

And I stand anxiously over the proving bowl
and wonder about the bread
what can I do to make it better?
How can I add something special?
I ruin it again and again with my striving.

But I have vowed to bake bread
and read this winter
and perhaps what I'm saying is
maybe I can teach myself
how to wait.

WHAT DOES YOUR HEART WANT AT THE CENTER OF YOUR LIFE?

plants and animals
homegrown food
hands
pleasure
trust
the way my body moves when I'm alone
the way the pen moves when an idea is pulling it, magnetic
allowing, not striving
but also some striving,
stretching, reaching,
not toward a goal, but toward the outstretched hand
sunlight
starlight
earth
poetry and words made round in the hollow of my mouth
a sense of fullness
the way a cheek fills the pillow or a child lies down in the center of
you before bedtime
travel, adventure, trains
coffee and a slowly moving mountain view
the moon
did I mention poetry?
and the way some things can only be understood in retrospect.

IF YOU ARE WHAT YOU LOVE THEN I AM...

the crackling of a campfire
the smell of rain
my son's infectious laughter
freshly baked bread with butter

I am flirtatious banter
getting to the heart of the thing
over cheese fries and milkshakes

I am road trips and mixtapes
the moon in all its phases
I am the deep ring of a cello
and swimming in warm water.

I am you, with your sweet eyes
and slow language.
I am the stars
this coffee
this life right here.

BELOW THE SURFACE

Love belongs to the darkest colors:
blues and purples so deep
they read as black.

Bodies move there like silk,
soft limbs slide past each other,
our bones now cartilage.

At night, I belong to no one and everyone.
I close my eyes and release the need to be separate,
release the illusion that we are apart.

HANDS OPEN

Do not underestimate
the power of simplicity,

of words told plainly
from a place deep inside

where the black waters
flow with the stories
of the future

where the mind melds
with earthstone

and foundations are built
on the fringes

where ancient secrets are
whispered only to

those who wait quietly
with hands open.

A THING WITH FUR

Do not imagine love
as a train
but as the air
in which the engine travels,

the water through which
everything flows,

the cells the universe uses
to make every kind
of sweet thing.

Love is the rising agent,
the spark,
the stomach flip,
the secret knowing,

the dream poem,
the softest kiss,

the endless fields
of lavender growing along
the emptiest of highways,

the burning sage
and the billy goat.

Love can be a thing
with fur, yes,

but not a thing with tracks.

It is everything
and anything
that moves freely.

BEING SEEN

I climb in through the open window
and sit perched like a raven.
claw my way inside
caw my way inside.

always a layer between us.

I know some people think
being invisible is a superpower
but so is being seen.
so is being seen.

LOST

Do you ever just stop
being able to see yourself?

Like some internal mirror
has been smashed
or perhaps you've grown

a new set of eyes and the
neural pathways no longer
connect to the place where
your "self" lives.

It is a groping for the light switch
a stumbling toward the locked car
a kind of lost that begs of you
the deepest levels of surrender.

The sundial won't work
underground. The compass
can't tell you which way is up.

NAKED

There is a writhing underneath
the skin of a poem

a longing that pulses
a bloodless, raging need

I can't sit still inside this breaking
push your words inside me
and ride them like fingers.

You wake at my trembling
I tremble at your inability
to control yourself.

Can you feel what's coming?

THINGS I WANT TO HOLD

I find myself seeking a sharpness
an arrow prick to the throat
or a perfectly ripe grapefruit

and I am either happy
or unconscionably sad

and the fact that I can't
tell the difference

reeks of trauma
but also maybe contentment?

And perhaps this is what rest feels like
like letting emotion go unnamed
but deeply felt in the body.

They never said this part
would be interesting,
I just assumed.

And now I want something
sharp to hold

like the hip of an ancient sea creature
or sand packed into a square
and filled with shark's teeth

The handles of a coin-operated tower-viewer

overlooking your childhood or

a basket you weaved from sweet grass
and remnants of your grandmother's nightgown

something to keep my mind
from eating itself
with boredom
or peace
or whatever we're calling this.

Sex or success
or fuck yes
or more texts

or possibly I could
just accept
that this is simply how it feels right now
empty-handed and
shock-less.

A sheer curtain drawn over
a gray day.

MOTHER WOUND

"You begin to heal yourself when you let go of the belief that you can save your mother." — Dan Booth Cohen

I want to wash my feet in the river
and walk naked in the desert
talking to coyote and the snake.
They have medicine and I have water
that I carried here in my mouth.

I have salt in my hands
and ash in my throat.
I burn the cities down
with my spleen and I have gathered
together the phoenixes for resurrection.

I am the wasting grasses,
the long tails of the peahens, uncolored and drab.
I am the blue-headed mallard
that floats by the boats in the Boston Garden lakes.

I bring destruction, fire.

My mother says the dandelions look like devastation
and I cannot understand her.
She speaks a foreign language
and everything tastes like soap
and feels like not being loved enough.

I grew up emaciated and grateful

for the bread crusts of attention
left over after her own trauma was tended to.

I am so tired of blaming her though,
we are two oak seeds caught in a tumble dryer.
No escape from the arid tossing.

I want to wash us both in the river
but she won't come.

And I have left her there,
dry and cracking, to save myself.
So that I might not borrow youth
from my own child.

I will heal and saturate,
soak up the water until I have a vessel to pour from,
and maybe then I can go back for her.

You do not need me
to teach you of your wild,
you need only to remember it.

Say your true name
quietly, under your breath.
Tell no one your secret.

JULY

Strong coffee
soft rain
weak knees
restraint

leave space
for interpretation.

take it all
slowly

train whistle
four kinds of   delays

don't let him
take you
for a ride

you drive, love
you drive.

SANDCASTLES

We were the most
beautifully constructed tower
just waiting
for the crushing sea.

and you smile
and tell me you miss me.

WILLING

In love with windows
and flower petals
skeleton keys and
antique door handles.
Hands
Hearts
Minds
I thrive on curiosity.
Give me anything that
opens willingly.

FOUND

I got so used to
finding the right buttons
to push, the correct
levers to pull.
How can I hold my body,
angle the camera,
phrase the boundary
to minimize my own
existence, to eliminate
the pieces of me
that repulse.

I got so used to
figuring out how
to make people love me
that I forgot how to
love myself.
Forgot how to discern
my own interest.
Forgot how to find
my way back home
afterward.

The path to self-erasure
was worn down to the pavement
while the path to self-expression
was covered with vines and thorns.

I tore myself to shreds

to be where I am,
standing in my garden
of wildflowers,
face to the sun,
more naked than nudity.
More whole than divided,
more found than lost.

Somehow, I am both
the horse and the rider
always falling off

chasing myself down.

wildly pursuing my own rhythm
my own strong hooves
drumming out percussive magic
on the dusty earth.

THE GOD COLOR

I would like to cover all
my sins in art and start again
as a palette of colors no one
has ever seen before.

Mantis shrimp colors,
the undersea colors that
only exist if you have extra cones.
Maybe the gods are in there,
shining and glorious,
everywhere,
sacred dust sparkling in a sunbeam.

If only you could see the God color

somewhere just north of orange
and slightly west of pink
like the sunset sometimes
when it's almost the ocean
and somehow also the desert.

UNANSWERABLE QUESTIONS

I am left groggy
and groping for words,

for a coherent way to say,
"I'm not sure if I love you
or I'm afraid of what I'll do
if I stay."

How many ways can I
take myself apart?

How many hands can you
put on me at once?

ASPEN

Do not mistake me
for an ingenue.
I am no blushing child,
no innocent lamb,

no orchid needing
just the right
kind of soil.

I am an aspen grove,
each stem connected
to the unseen whole,

a multitude of selves,
exploring the world
in one body.

I am so much harder to love than I first seem.

A DANGEROUS WOMAN

My power resides
somewhere deeper
than my beauty now,
in my brazen authenticity,
my fearless freedom,
my deviant claiming
of my own autonomy.

I have learned to say
"I love you" to the mirror
and mean it.
Really mean it.

And there's nothing
more dangerous than that.

THE SAGE

I have so much sage
and not enough wisdom.

I am always forgetting
to rest. I am always
trying to please some
invisible disciplinarian,

slap my own wrists
with the ruler and
cry out for a moment
alone to get myself

together. To burn away
this secret fear that
I will never stop
treating myself

as someone who has
to continually earn
her keep.

INNER VOICE

She is meant to see
the quiet things,
to remind you of them
softly

like the sun thawing
ice, like the moon's
slow drift from the
horizon

like the familiar melody
played almost imperceptibly
that reminds you of a time
you can taste with your
mind's eye but know you'll
never see.

MARILYN

I have this thing for trains,
not real trains as much,
but imaginary ones
in black and white movies,
red lipstick, cocktail dresses.

I am Marilyn Monroe
smoking a cigarette off the back car
and I am the man trying to kiss her.
I can feel her small frame,
curvy and warm under my hands
and I touch my hair slicked back
with shoe polish.

I grew up on old movies,
the chemistry and banter
makes real life feel sluggish
and underwater.

I crave that crisp clarity of wit,
that choice turn of phrase,
the ease of bursting into song.
Soft film edges,
blurred and drunk.

I kiss you
down to the couch
and let the screen
fade to black.

KATHARINE HEPBURN

It's always been Katharine, with her
long pants and masculine eyebrows.
Her ability to say what she meant
in a room full of men.

I miss her like a sister I never
had and I want her like a woman

I've never had.
I picture the
banter and the '40s era bathing

suits and I realize I've never been
straight for a single day but wanting
to be *with* someone
and wanting to *be* them

are such indistinguishable states
until they are not.
I look into the black and white
screen and see myself at
10 finding all the ways it might've been.

I am made of honesty these days
simple and plain
as the cold morning light.
like heartbeat
like exhales
like gold.

AUGUST

August reminds us
that we are all the sea
in human form,
just salt and water
in motion.

It's hard to be mad
at the world in August,
better to swim naked
under summer skies
and stay right
in the heart of now.

PNEUMA

It's time to let the ocean into your hair,
time to let the salt out of your lungs.
It's time to drift in and out
on breath-like waves,
to see the jellyfish belly
and make her your friend.

It's time to open every treasure chest
filled with your own capacity
to see yourself as others do:
with generosity and awe.

Close every door that tries to ensnare you
into one kind of person.

TIME WITCH

My heart is an
anachronism
beating in every
century at once.

a ticking mess of
ventricles and ash,
burned at the stake

too many times to count.

(sometimes I miss people
I've never met
from timelines
I can only visit in my dreams)

NOSTALGIA

I wish you could photograph
the way a place smells:

of woodfire and lilac
of warm earth and freedom

of ancient memories
you're not quite ready for.

NO DIVING

She is the reef
and the sharks,
beautiful and treacherous.

Not all waters
have a safe side.

40

Bright cheeks and worn hands,
this is as good as it gets.
The perfect blend of maturity
and vitality with just a hint
of rebellion.

Let this be the moment
of your becoming, love.

Proclaim yourself ready.

You are so beautiful
when you're not
breaking my heart.

And sometimes,
even then.

We climb inside each other,
eternal children
playing adults.

And sometimes it aches
like snakes
trying to put
their skins back on.

IF YOU ARE WHAT YOU LOVE, PART II

I am leather boots
and old books,

film camera clicks
and charcoal-stained fingers.

I am Wite-Out and
vintage typewriters,

always making mistakes,
always willing to show up
anyway.

I am sacred spaces,

a room growing calmer,

a child finding her
true voice.

I am the moon
moving in tandem
with the earth,

the wolf howling,

the rows of teeth
in a white shark's grin.

I am the ocean,
painfully deep,
mournfully indigo.

But mostly I am trees,

I am always,
always trees.

If you could
just come here
and say my name
very close to my ear

I am sure the heat of us
would set the world

on fire.

SEPTEMBER

Fall breezes and summer light,
September is the ripe apple
we wait all year for,
the crush of joy so sweet
we know it cannot last.

I tremble with the still green leaves,
both of us knowing
it's only a matter of time now.

September is the prayer
for presence
within the dazzling ache
of unsustainable beauty.

AGAIN AND AGAIN I CHOOSE AUTUMN

I breathe in a new vision
of coming home full,
of finding peace on the
inside of things.
To drop into my life,
to drop into it fully.

All of my autumns
are a way of sinking further
into intuition, into a deep knowing
that adventure lives inside me,
inside you, inside the space between
our bodies, the channels we unlock
with our writing, our songs,
the paintings are impressionists.

We come together in dreams and art
to reveal what we already know:

there is no such thing
as disconnection,

just cycles and seasons
of coming and going
ebbing and flowing
waxing and waning
drifting closer and closer
to the truth
with each passing year.

THE CIRCLE

Where are the people
who stay up late
and need the moon?

Who let their stories
drip blood truths into
dark, moist nightscapes?

Let's find each other
and speak only of the ways
we can remember ourselves free.

FALL IS FOR WRITERS

The sound of typewriters
and the smell of freshly brewed coffee,
soft sweaters and gray cats.

Autumn is the time for writers,
for dreamers, for philosophers
and bakers, for artists and singers,
for healers and teachers.

For all of us with sensitive
nervous systems and way too
much empathy...

For anyone who waits all year
for the world to settle down
so they can remember who
they are.

Liminal creatures who love
the moon, who crave the sea,
who ache for forest cover
and candlelight.

Fall is for magic,
for intuition,
for release.

COAL MINE

I write poems
while you
run circles
around me.

The canary
flees
your chaotic
movements —
a warning
I should
probably heed.

You are not safe
but when has
that ever
stopped me?

MORNING CROWS

Every time I lose confidence
in my work, I remember that
I am allowed to write in my
own voice.

I am allowed to
write about my own life
even if the voices
of doubt are morning crows
at my window.

Even if my stomach
is eating itself and
the dangerous thoughts
flow out of the corners
like spiders carrying
scissors.

I gather these
sharp things

and return to the page.
More cutting. Less safe.

ARS POETICA

The life of a writer
is a tricky
combination
of recklessness
and discipline,
just chaos held
together
with bits of
fraying yarn,
butterflies
pinned to the board
still fluttering.

An impossible
attempt
to capture
what still moves.

I KEEP TRYING TO WRITE ABOUT INFINITY

instead of remembering that awe is invoked

in tiny moments we can picture
with our mind's eye:

My dog trotting joyfully on frozen leaves.

The nest I found, filled with seeds,
hidden in the red berry bush.

The bare branches of the winter willow
shining in the sunlight on Hawthorn Street.

My ears hurt from the cold
and my teeth protest the hot coffee
after my frigid morning stroll.

But my mind is clear and still
as the mystic lake

and I have remembered how to
survive another day.

No poet ever writes a book
because the world is beautiful.

They use beauty to pull you in,
to make you see

how this gorgeous garden
has stung them

until the words,
still and quiet on the page,
are the only way to breathe.

I AM A CREATURE OF AUTUMN

A red fox crunching leaves beneath black paws.
The hawk circling around for hours.

I am falling oak leaves,
the cooler rustling winds.
I am the hollow in the tree being filled with acorns.

I am the turning on the axis,
the downside of the hill,
the way everything slides more quickly
into darkness, into rest.

I am the open windows
and the hot steam rising.

You already know I am the fire crackling,
the stew brewing.

I am the soft way the locket snaps closed.
I am the clacking of the typewriter keys.

I am adding another quilt to the end of the bed,
just in case.
I am the warm body ready to hold you closer.

I am a creature of the autumn,
my blue eyes shine brighter in the dark.

WE ARE FOUND IN THE LEAST HOLY OF PLACES

I am picturing an alley,
lit only by the half-full moon.

I am picturing the glow of neon fish.

I am picturing the way our eyes see the clock
in the hotel room and have to place
a washcloth over it to sleep.

I am picturing the desert
with its pink-soft edges
and its shaking dangerous rattle tails.

I am thinking of how I couldn't stand
the feeling of always being thirsty
for green.

I am thinking of how holy the trees
and water feel to my cracked feet
and how I know that even now,
in this pandemic,
I have see how divine threads
connect and embolden the smallest
hints of hope,

like moon,
like fluorescence,
like rain.

I wake some days
and see a new face
in the mirror
and wonder
what soft shift
was born
in the darkness
of night?

OH, OCTOBER!

you feel like my heart,
exploding with color
and ready to let go
of everything that
wants to fall away.

THE ACHE

I keep looking over at him
just to remind myself what he looks like,

just to ease the ache of not looking at him.

Like tears you can feel coming by
the tightening in your throat, he is
a stretching that nothing can relieve

but the sweet pressure of his body
and the look on his face that reassures me

that I'm not the only one
who loves so hard it hurts.

BOUNDARIES

I take back my breath
I take back my heart
my time, my attention
my easy intuition.

I take back my smile
and my specific way
of seeing the best in you.

Tuck them into my pockets
with the smooth stones I collected
from the river.

I have many gifts
for those who choose to stay
and none for those who walk away.

TABULA RASA

I sometimes want to start over fresh,
blank page, white field,
new name, new life.
Not just a new country
but an entirely new universe.

I believe I have done this many times.
I can feel them all stacked on each other,
worlds like Jenga pieces,
falling, collapsing, and overlapping.

This day, I have lived it before,
only this time I will throw the stone
into the lake and watch my reflection
scatter into rings that vibrate out
into the echoing universe.

This time I will choose me
and I will choose freedom
and I will choose joy.

SENSITIVE BODIES ARE ONLY GOOD FOR POETRY.

Poetry and shallow rivers with gray stones
to stand on, even though it hurts.

Poetry and the way lavender looks growing
along the highway, just a blur of purple you
try, in vain, to capture with your phone.

Poetry and the way the light falls
in his bedroom in long,
orange rectangles on languid,
intertwining legs.

Poetry and horses
grazing in morning mists,
that smell after it rains,
or the sting of hot water on bare skin.

Poetry and the hoot of barn owls,
the sound of heels on cobblestone,
and laughter bouncing off galaxies.

Just poetry and the slowly burrowing ache of beauty.

YOU BECOME A METAPHOR

I let you silence me
over and over again.

You stop being a man
and become a metaphor
for every man,

for my father
for God
even my own son.

I become a goddess,
angry and incensed
at my willingness
to play along

in my own shrinking.
Narrow eyes and
shredded pulse,

I walk away
before I do something
you might regret.

DIANA

I will call her Diana
I will call her the muse
I will call her Artemis
Moon huntress
Love of my life.
She will cast arm spells
the ones that look like urns
the ones that turn my guts
to fire, one look spins
me into a maelstrom of
desire.
I wait in the darkness
for her to take my hand
and guide me to the places
where men aren't allowed to go.
To the sea caves
to the warm, wet den
to the inside places
where it smells of blood
and life.

WHEN YOU LACK INSPIRATION

Take a deep breath
and ease into the
tepid water of boredom.
Allow it to soak into
your bones, do not fear
the emptiness.

Creativity needs this
open space, discomfort,
lack.

It is here, in the malaise,
that true genius is hiding,
waiting for her time to shine.

Shhh now, she is almost
brave enough to come out now.

Stay patient.
Stay still.

BURN SAGE UNTIL YOU'RE WHOLE AGAIN.

Step quietly upon the moss that grows
in the darkest parts of the elm woods,
bare toes find soft patches
among the stones.

Tend the fire with dreams
that crackle like twigs in the flames,
faint glimmers of all your lives
float up, shining, into the atmosphere.

The stars look down in envy
at this symphony of animation.
To live just one day with kisses.
Your hands, your mouth,
your soft hair and human heart.

A NEW LANDSCAPE

Just give me a train ticket,
an open window,
a cup of tea,
and an unknown landscape.
The rest will take
care of itself.

OCTOBER 9, 2021

My dad is dead
and the reflected trees look like orange paint in the water
my dad died today
and there are mushrooms everywhere
my dad had a heart attack
and the air smells like campfire and pine
my dad and I will never sing harmony again
and my child is poking the water with a stick
my dad died and I didn't say goodbye

The crows are talking to each other about the coming winter
my dad died
and the women are angry that my dog is off his leash

I dreamt about him two nights ago
woke today with a strange feeling
that I was forgetting something important.

HALF OF YOU

I don't want to look at myself
afraid I'll see the absence of you
afraid you're all I'll see.

I carry so much of who you are within me
pile sandbags around the inherited traits
the way we both flit from lover to lover
or change careers near constantly.

The way we dream too big
the way it hurts all the time
able to talk to anyone yet
always feeling alone.

I draw lines down the middle of my body
to remind myself I only carry half your DNA
and maybe I can bypass the bits of you
that operate only in shadow.

Your own father died when you were 12
and you were raised by your brothers.
You sang and drank
and pulled women towards you
like every cigarette in a carton.

I watched you exhale your bravado
into the cold Illinois air
your eyes gazing out at the distance.

And I miss only how our voices knew
how to harmonize into one
indistinguishable noise.

THE YEAR

It has been the year of aching quietly,
the year of roses,
the year of bread-making and heartbreaking,
and fearing the tickle in the back of your throat.
It has been a year of bad watercolor art
and putting your hand out the car window
to remember the taste of the wind.

It has been the year of missing:
missing travel,
missing hugs,
missing grocery store smiles.

It has been a year of rediscovering who I am
at my quietest, my most unfiltered, my most afraid.
It has been a year of letting go,
of holding on,
of apathy and desperation.
It has been a year of death,
external bodies dropping,
refrigerated trucks waiting to take them away.
Internal, childhood: on pause,
learning to swim: on pause,
making a friend: on pause.

It has been *the* year,
do you know what I mean?
The one they'll write about in the history books,
the one we will try to forget.

THE WAY OF SOFT THINGS

It's okay if you crave
belonging and solitude
at once,
if you don't know
what you need right now.

Take it slowly,
pay attention,
stand alone in the warm
morning light.

Expand into the world
and then contract.

This is the way of everything soft:

like breathing
like seasons
like tides.

THREE INCHES OF WATER

Some days are just
wet carpet in the basement
and a slowly crushing ache
in the chest.

Sometimes grief lives
in your bones and makes
your brain feel like
an enemy.

It's okay to be sad
for no discernible reason.
Joy comes that way, too.

Every time I feel abandoned
by someone, it is likely more
true to say that I have
abandoned myself,
disappeared again
into the dream
of never feeling alone.

TOO SOFT

If I'm not careful
I can let the world consume me

with its prying eyes and pointless conversations.
I try so hard to understand

but I don't understand.
This racing around,
this striving for gold,

piles and piles like dragons
whose breaths become paper

and whose hearts turn to banks
filled with gemstones.

I am so soft.
Too soft for this hard business.

I let my sugar cube eyes melt in the morning sun
and I sink, sweet and quiet,
into my own small world.

TOO LATE

The glass shatters the silence
of this strange decade we're in and
I keep forgetting what year it is,
keep forgetting where I put my hands,
how to hold this life now that it's in tatters,
old fabric scraps you find
under the sink left by the previous owners.

We are all in our front lawns
searching for the source of sound,
an accident, a baseball through a window,
another mother left childless,
another child left motherless,
and still we turn our car radios up
and listen to the DJs tell their awful jokes.

We don't know how to hold this much destruction at once,
rush back to what was.
How do we stay safe when we can't huddle together?
When huddling together is definitionally not safe?

Everything terrible overflowing
onto the dance floor like confetti
that chokes the birds.

We learn everything too late.
We learn everything too late.

I am in the trees again.
They grow bare and thin like me
full of shadow and creaking
whistling wind and whispers

we are cold and still
we are hungry for the sun.

NOVEMBER

There's a bittersweet poignancy
to this time of year, a beauty
so ripe with flavor,
it almost hurts the soul.

I stand in the yard, sun baking my back,
eating the last of the summer blackberries
and listening to the birds.

They are discussing
the coming journey:
Will they leave today
or tomorrow?

And who will they be
upon the return?

THIS IS HOW YOU DO IT

You take the next step
into the unknown.
My love, you listen so closely
to the voice that whispers
sweet words in the morning dark,
before the sun lifts her head
from the horizon, before your son
lifts his head from the dinosaur pillowcase.

This is how you do it: slowly, deliberately,
one page and then another.
You stop trying so hard,
let the pen run loosely over the page,
let the fingers trace gently over the skin.

You feel into the blank spaces.
Let silence have a deep hold
on the rhythm.
Let breath be equal to words.

This is how you do it —
you simply get out of your own way
over and over again.

Follow, flow, surrender.
And when the creative miracle kisses you
you kiss back.

You always kiss back.

PERMISSION TO FEEL

There is sun and hot tea.
There are clean sheets
and people who love me.

There is a heart beating in my chest,
A brain working overtime
to stay here in the present.

There is grief and anxiety.
There is fatigue and tedium.
Time moves strangely,
in fits and starts.

This moment
This day
These feelings
This ache that is both
profound gratitude and immense dread...

It is all allowed.
It is all here to remind me that I am alive.

ADVICE FOR SAD DAYS

clean your space
and take a bath
drink some water
and listen to music from your adolescence.
Sit in the sun
eat something green
tell someone you love them
say "thank you" to yourself in the mirror
remove one thing from your calendar
go to bed a little early tonight.
I love you
you're so brave
little by little the poison inside you
will seep into the ground

breathe in safety
breathe out fear

breathe in love
breathe out anger

breathe in acceptance
breathe out avoidance

breathe
breathe
breathe

CREATE SOMETHING NEW:

A pattern, a recipe, a story, a poem.
Plant a seed, be metaphorical.
Now is not the time to be boring.
Get inventive, get bold, get weird and outlandish.
Get uncomfortably vulnerable.

Construct a new status quo,
figure out your deepest,
wildest, most expansive dreams for the world
and write them down, build them up.
Begin. Conceive. Create. Birth. Open.

If ever there was a time for you to become
who you always dreamed you could be, it is now,
when the rules are soft and edges are blurred
and the world is blinking into an uncertain future.

Be the future that comes into sharp focus.
Tell the truth. The absolute truth.
Spare none of the details.
The only way through this is
mutually assured creation.

YOU HAVE TO TRUST ME

(I know what I'm talking about)

New things are good for the brain.
New skin, new touch, new views,
new faces, new hearts, new blood,
new aches, new discomforts,
new awkwardness,
new orgasms.

You learn by doing.
You create life by
experiencing it.

We are not here to work.
We are not here to just survive.
We are here to play, to dance,
to make love, to eat,
to pray, to cry, to try
to mother,
to taste the wild berries
and sleep under the stars,
to feel the sun and the rain
and the newly formed love
that radiates between two
very old souls.

TETHER ME TO FINITE MOMENTS

You untangle my thoughts
like you are brushing
my deeply knotted hair:

gently at first,
subtle questions
and a tugging intuition.

Tending to the tender parts
with the most care

until my brow is smoothed
and your hands run freely
through my synapses.

Drag your fingers
through my thoughts
and tell me I'm yours.

Everything eventually dissolves,
even these borders between us.

UNSTOPPABLE

Move toward people who smile
when they see you,
not from politeness,
but from the inside, unstoppably emerging
like butterflies from the mouth.

Move toward people who move you
from the inside.

Play drums until the concrete grief
begins to crack and moss grows in the creases.
Get softer and softer
until floating seems inevitable,
until you are dandelion seeds,
rain,
sand,
molecules,
birds
flying in loops that look like cream
dancing in black coffee.

Loosen your edges
until you are no longer alone,
until you feel a connection
with the paper and pen,
the table,
the dog softly breathing,
the self you forget who lives forever.

Trust me,
you are not alone.
You are everything good.
Everything free.

HOPE

Hope wafts in one evening.
I can track her scent on
twilight breezes like
freshly baked cherry pie
on windowsills
or newly blooming
lilac bushes.

I welcome her in
with camomile tea
and vanilla cake,
my honored guest
after weeks of hosting
only grief.

PICK UP THE ASHES OF TIME

and hold them gently
under moonlight —
their flicker will alight
your soul with intention.

Blow gently to release yourself
from ancient patterns,
the ones your grandmother
bakes with, the ones you ate up
like snow cones from your childhood.

Let the burning begin
at the cellular level,
take hot baths to
soak up the trauma.

Allow this year to remind you
where it hurts, to light up your
inner guidance system
like tiny emergency airplane lights.
Move quietly toward the nearest exit.

You carry your own salvation
in your bones, simply deploy
the parachute and fly,
phoenix hatchling,
toward another kind of fire.

AFTERMATH

Sometimes you find a cashmere sweater
the color of your eyes
at a thrift store in the Haight
and you bring it home like
an embrace you can wear.

Sometimes you have a simple conversation
with a shuttle driver from the airport
in St. Louis and burst into tears at the kindness,
the Midwestern humanity of the exchange.

Sometimes you drive through the cornfields
you drove through in the '90s
and remember the land as much as the man.
How the neatly planted rows
make patterns as you drive past.
Sacred geometry.

Sometimes you wander through the Fells
and listen to your child finding sticks
that look like boomerangs,
turning everything into weapons
despite your best attempts to foster peace in the world.

Sometimes it all aches,
the strange way things come together:
beauty and heartbreak
death and memory
love and grief.

SWEET POTATOES

The sweet potatoes have leaked
sweet juices onto the oven floor,
baking to charred, bubbling,
sticky, smoking puddles of tar.

I am scraping at the residue
and wondering how I forget
that this happens every time.

I am not very good at certain things.
Household chores hold little
romance for me and I will hole
up in my room for days
with the laptop on my comforter,
and piles of empty fizzy water cans.

Some days I barely see my child,
and he calls out my name as I descend
the staircase like I am a long lost aunt
or a friend he hasn't seen in years.

As I take his face in my hands,
my heart melts sweet juices
into the sole of my shoes
and every tasty thing about me
turns to black ash
and I vow once again
to show up for my life.

NOW

I don't know
where my head is
but the light in the branches
of the neighbor's tree
is a perfect shade of longing.

you say that time
is running out
but darling, look
at this morning —
look what we have,

it's everything
everything.

ACKNOWLEDGMENTS

A huge thank you to everyone who made this book possible. Unspeakable gratitude for my husband, John, for his unwavering love and support, for enabling me to pursue this career, for showing me what fatherhood can look like, and for being a true partner in this life. For my child, Quillen, who is the bravest, funniest, most authentic person I know. I love you so much. For David, who helps me ask the most interesting questions, who sees me with a kind of compassion and acceptance that makes me a better person every day. I wouldn't be a writer without you. Another giant thank you to my parents, Patricia and Charles, who gave me my appreciation for the written word, who revere art and music, who made a living of reading and deeply drawing meaning from text. Thank you for always being there for me. Writing would be a lonely endeavor if it weren't for my incredible poetry community and mentors — you know who you are. I love you all so much. Thank you more specifically to my financial supporter, Michael J; my publisher, Michelle Halket at Central Avenue; my editor, Beau Avery Adler; and everyone who worked on this book to make it a reality. I am deeply grateful.

Alix Klingenberg is a poet, spiritual director, and creative dilettante. She describes herself as a cross between an ancient woodland creature and an alternative '90s girl stereotype and is only half-kidding. Alix graduated from Oberlin College with a degree in visual art where she studied film and photography. She also has a master of divinity (multi-class bard/cleric anyone?). Alix lives near Boston, MA, with her family, 2 black cats, and a ridiculous dog named Cricket. She is queer and polyamorous, and has a passion for social justice, intersectional feminism, community, and the natural world. You can find more of her poetry and art on Instagram @AlixKlingenberg.

2023

Published by Central Avenue Poetry, an imprint of Central Avenue Marketing Ltd.
www.centralavenuepublishing.com

BREAD SEX TREES

Trade Paperback: 978-1-77168-358-6
EPUB: 978-1-77168-359-3

Published in Canada
Printed in United States of America

1. POETRY / Women   2. POETRY / Subjects & Themes - Nature

1 3 5 7 9 10 8 6 4 2

Keep up with Central Avenue